WONDERFUL HANDMADE LAMPS-HOME DECOR

SANDEEPA BHATIA

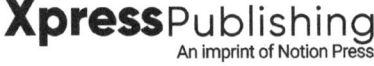
XpressPublishing
An imprint of Notion Press

XpressPublishing
An Imprint of Notion Press

No.8, 3rd Cross Street,CIT Colony,
Mylapore, Chennai, Tamil Nadu-600004

ISBN 978-1-63606-504-5

TO MOM & DAD,

WHO ALWAYS INPIRED ME WITH THEIR EXPERIENCES

LOVE & DEDICATION

LOVE YOU MOM & DAD ALWAYS ....

Contents

Foreword

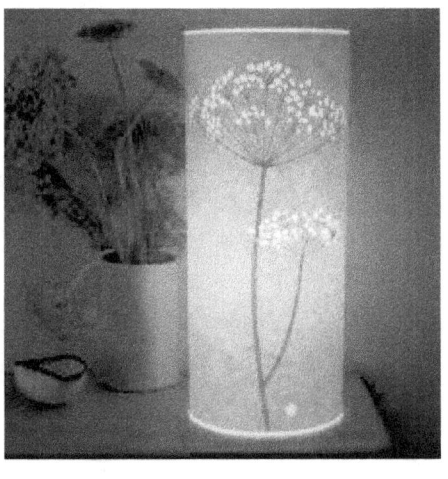

HANDMADE PAPER LAMP

This inspiring, tantalizing project book shines a light on the most artistic, well made, innovative, and beautiful lamps you can now make yourself. Bursting with many gorgeous photographs to spark your creativity, as well as a multitude of tried-and-true tips and ideas, Wonderful Handmade Lamps features 10 contemporary projects presented in useful step-by-step tutorials. The tutorials make it easier than you would ever imagine! In addition to the huge, pictorial lamps gallery, which will fuel your own ideas,Wonderful Handmade Lamps provides comprehensive techniques you need to know to construct stunning lamp designs that are fundamentally sound.

Preface

Lamps are the light and life of every room. Discover how easy it is to enhance your rooms with this complete introduction to the art of making BEAUTIFUL HANMADE LAMPS. Many creative project ideas are presented in this illuminating book. You will learn how to cover, line, and trim an existing lamps, as well as create your own distinctive lamps and shades in a variety of stunning styles. Clear, concise, and easy to follow instructions and illustrations will make it easy. For the designer and decorator, the silhouettes of lamps are named and defined. A section shows you how each base and shade complement each other, so you can combine them using good design techniques. Learn how you can change the look of a room instantly with the versatility of lamps. And if you are interested in selling your wares, a section on pricing your work is included. This comprehensive how-to will inspire everyone

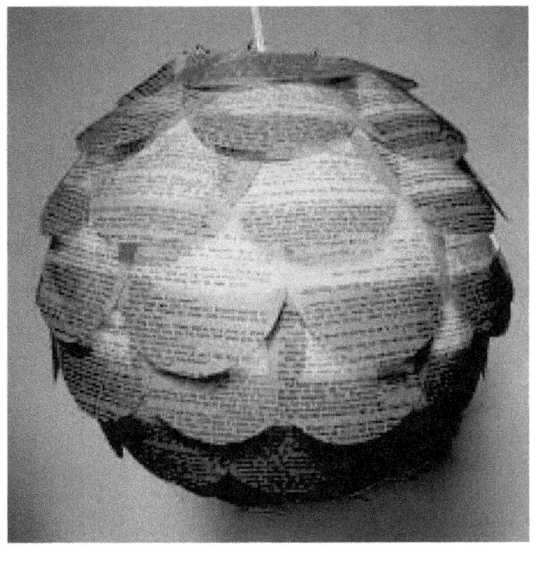

NEWSPAPER HAMDMADE LAMPS

Acknowledgements

Beautiful Designs to Illuminate Your Home.Here are some ideas for DIY lamps for your next craft or home decor project! ... All the tutorial here! are Amazing &innovative ! ... Adorable Handmade.These currently made beautiful lamps are nearly as cool as this custom lamp, crafted with care .The illuminated minds to illuminate your next inovation for creating Beautiful Handmade lamps .....So keep CREATING.......

Prologue

Searching for handmade and fair-trade gifts to give to family and friends? This Book offer a stunning selection of lamps,janhing lamps, scorner lamps, table lamps, and more! ... Wonderful Handmade Lamps-Home Decor.

DIY projects on :, Hanging Lamps, and More With Handmade Garden lamp Projects also .

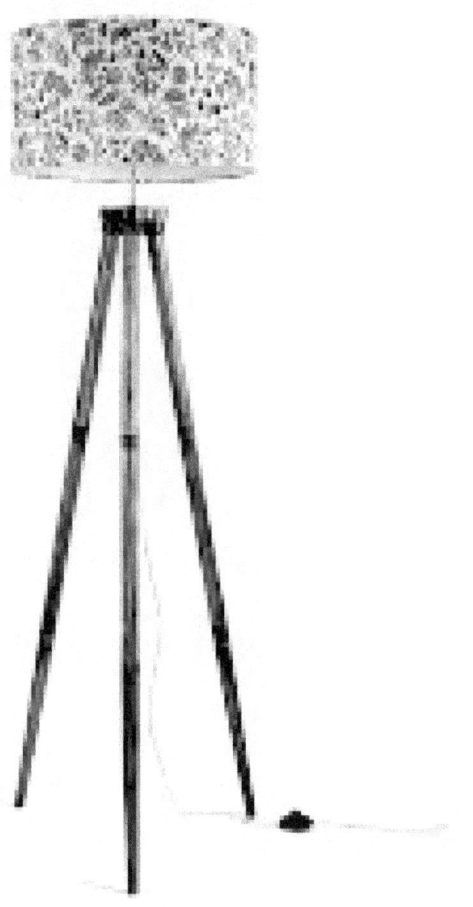

Handmade Standing lamp

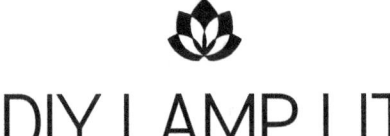

CHAPTER ONE

DIY LAMP LIT

DIY LAMP KIT

Beautiful designer lamps can cost hundreds of dollars. With a DIY kit, you'll be able to make a beautiful, quality lamp for a fraction of the cost. You'll also be able to perfectly match your lamp to your own style and decor needs. We all have different taste - don't settle for a generic lamp. Make a lamp you love!

Follow along in the pictures below as I go through the the individual components that make up a lamp and how to wire a lamp from scratch. Or keep scrolling down for step-by-step instructions on how to make a table or floor lamp, using pretty much anything as a base. And when you're done, you'll never think of wiring a lamp as a scary project ever again!

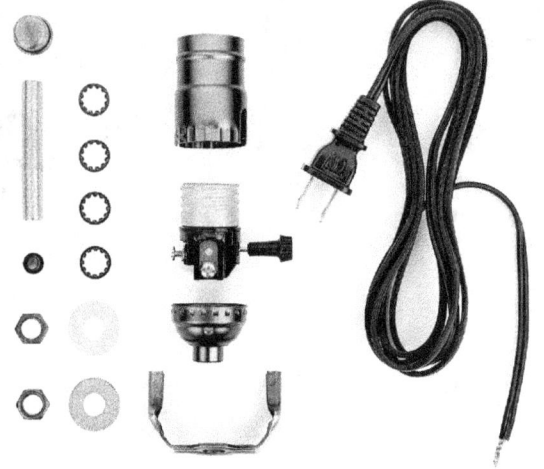

DIY LAMP KIT

LAMP KIT BEFORE MAKING FINAL LAMP

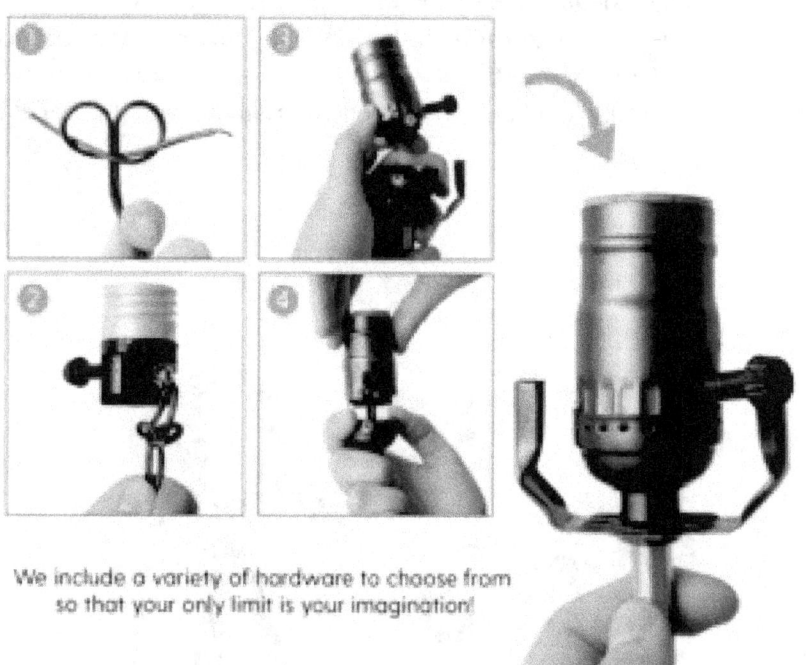

STEP BY STEP INSTRUCTIONS TO FIX SOCKET FOR BULB

LAMP MAKING KIT

WHAT'S INCLUDED?

A. 3 Piece Antique Brass Socket Set with Standard On-Off Knob

B. 12 Ft Long Brown Cord (18-gauge, SPT-2 2-conductor)

C. Saddle (for attaching a lamp harp / lampshade)

D. Threaded Steel Pipe

E. Rubber - Knurl Washers

F. 2 x Rubber Washers

G. Black Bushing

H. 4 x Lockwashers

I. 2 x Locknuts

J. Antique Brass Finial with Standard Threading

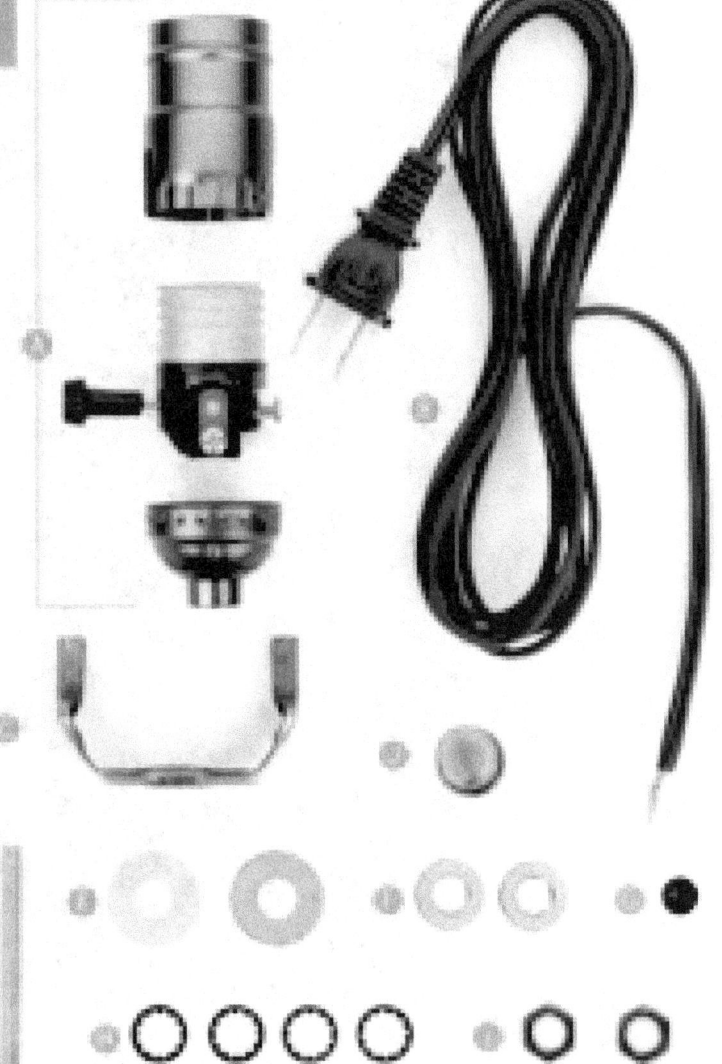

This Set Includes One Lamp Kit for Making a DIY Lamp

WINE BOTTLE LAMP

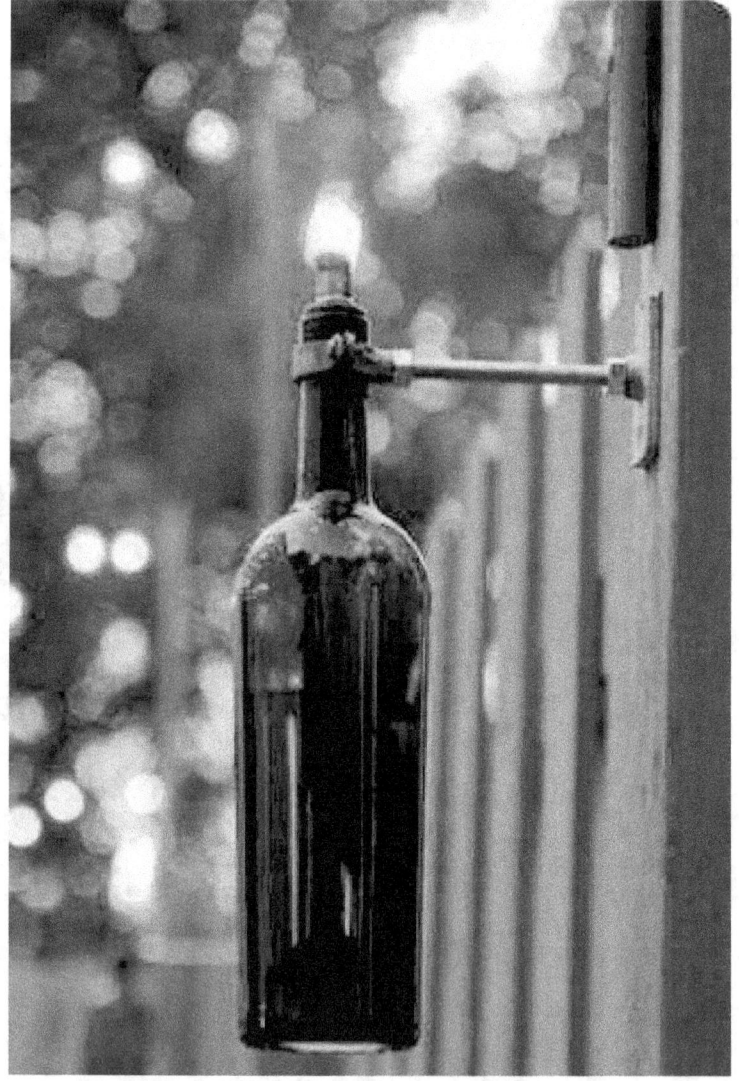

WINE BOTTLE LAMP

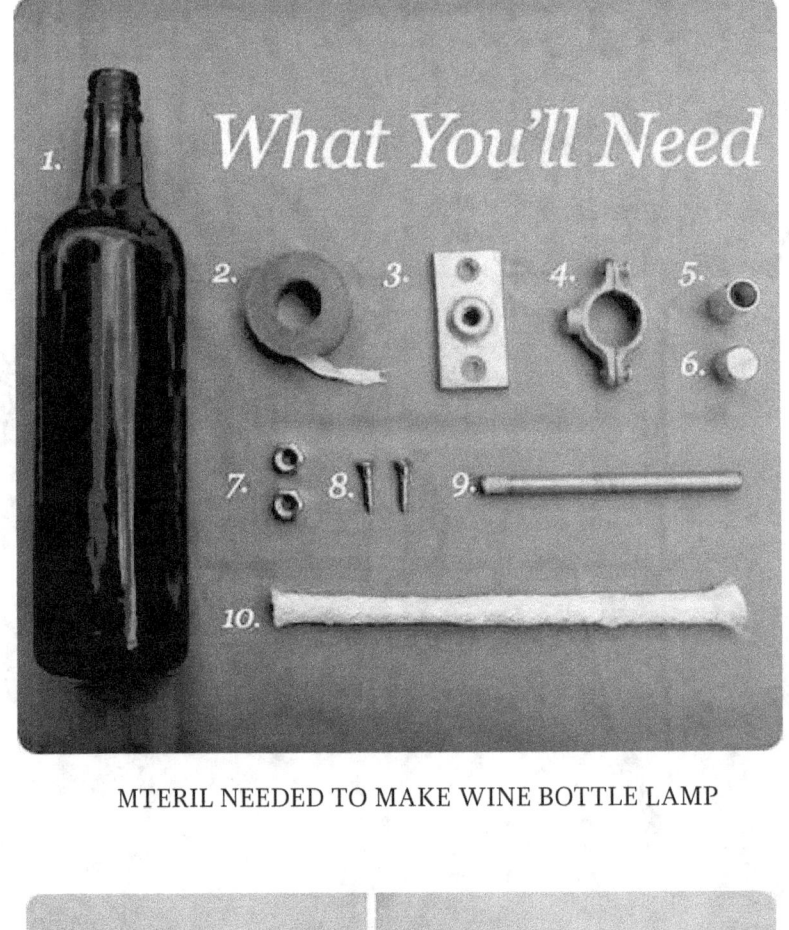

MTERIL NEEDED TO MAKE WINE BOTTLE LAMP

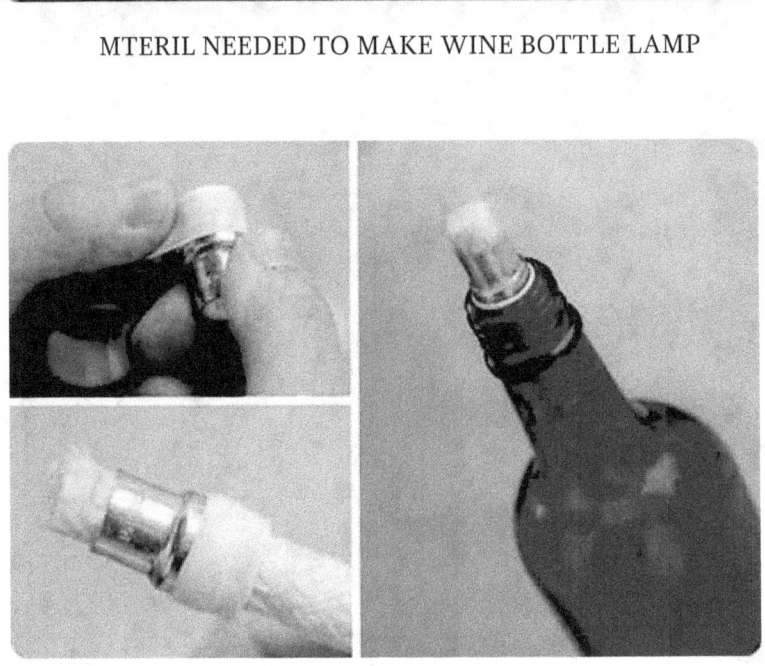

WICK FOR THE BOTTLE LAMP

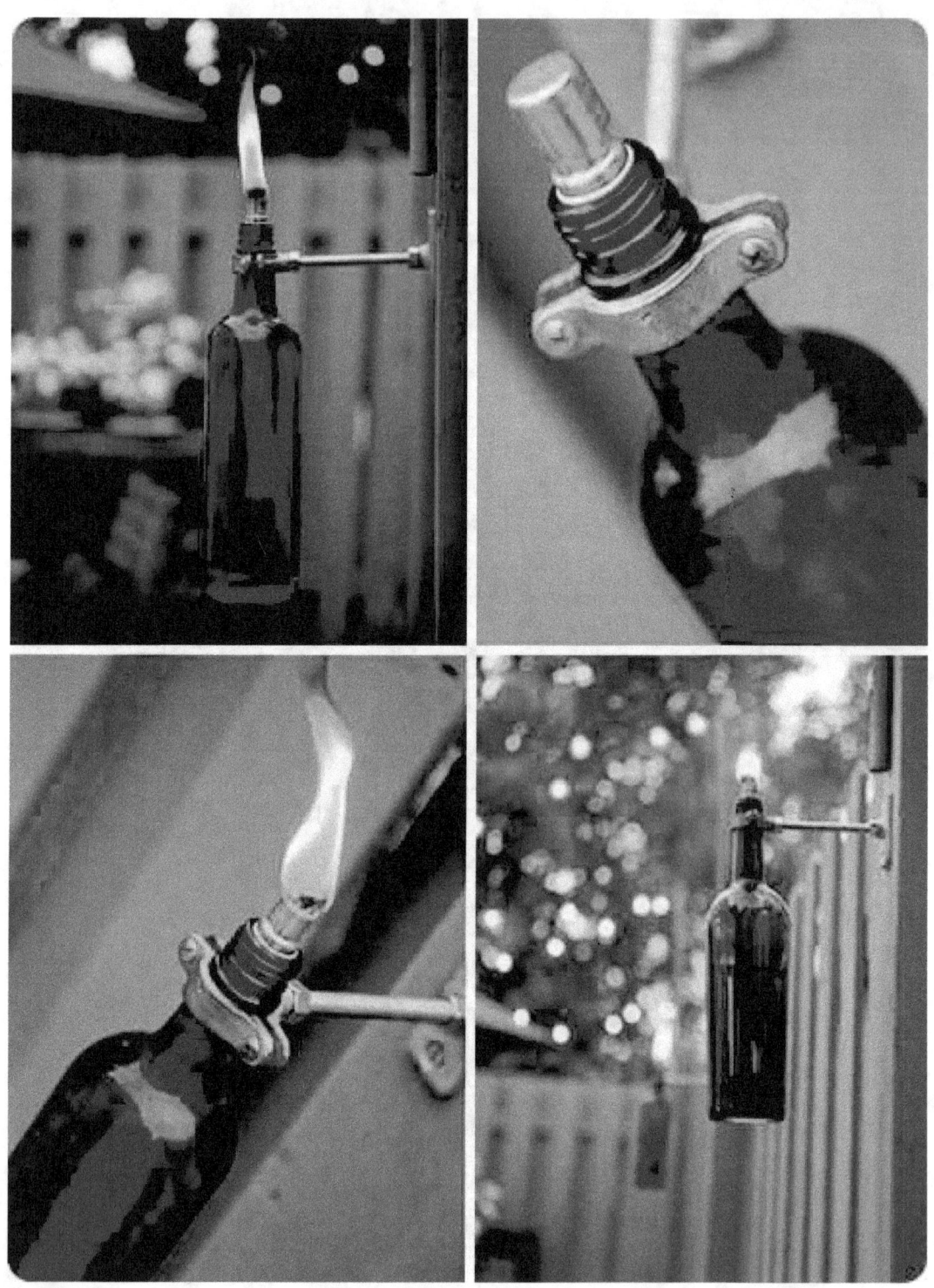

FINAL LAMP ADJUSTMENTS

TULLE PENDANT LAMP

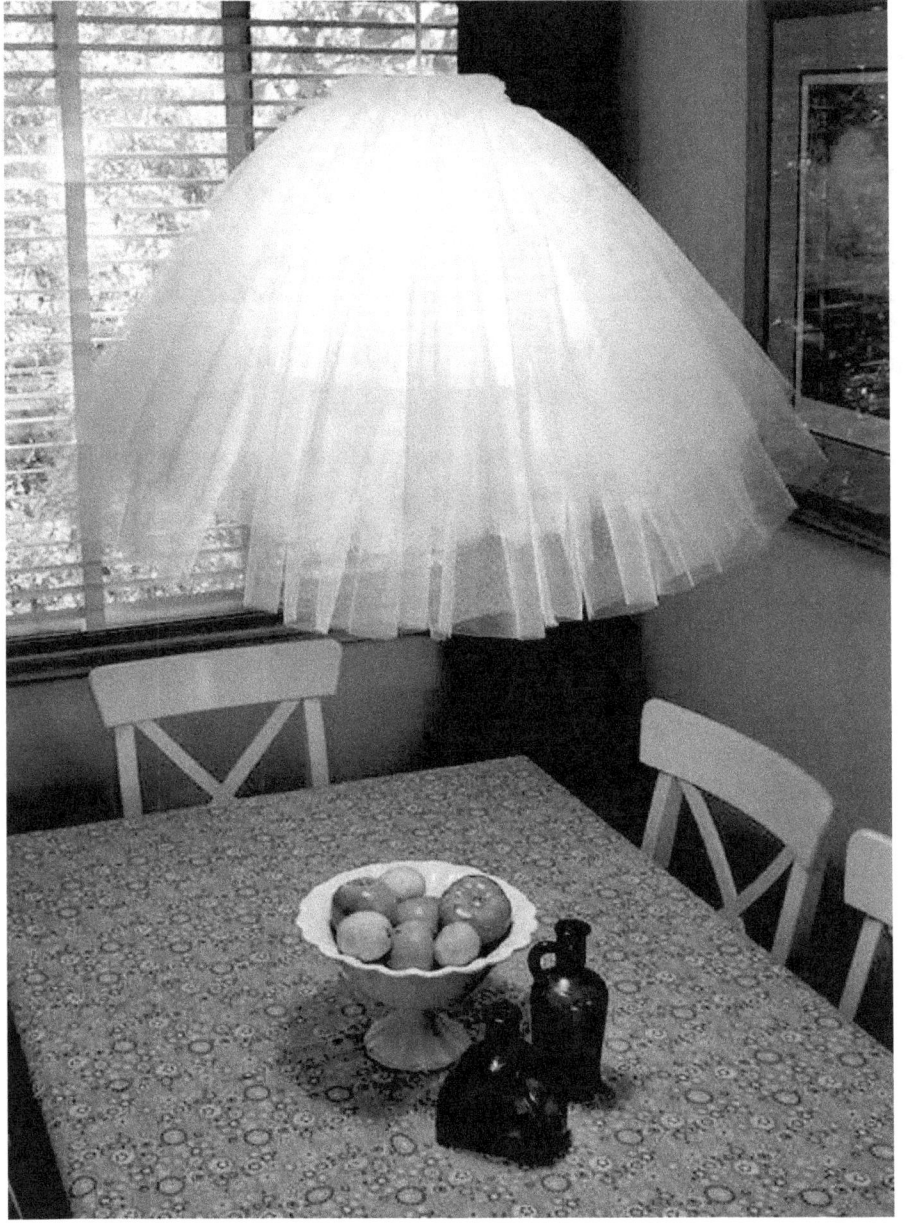

TULLE PENDANT LAMP

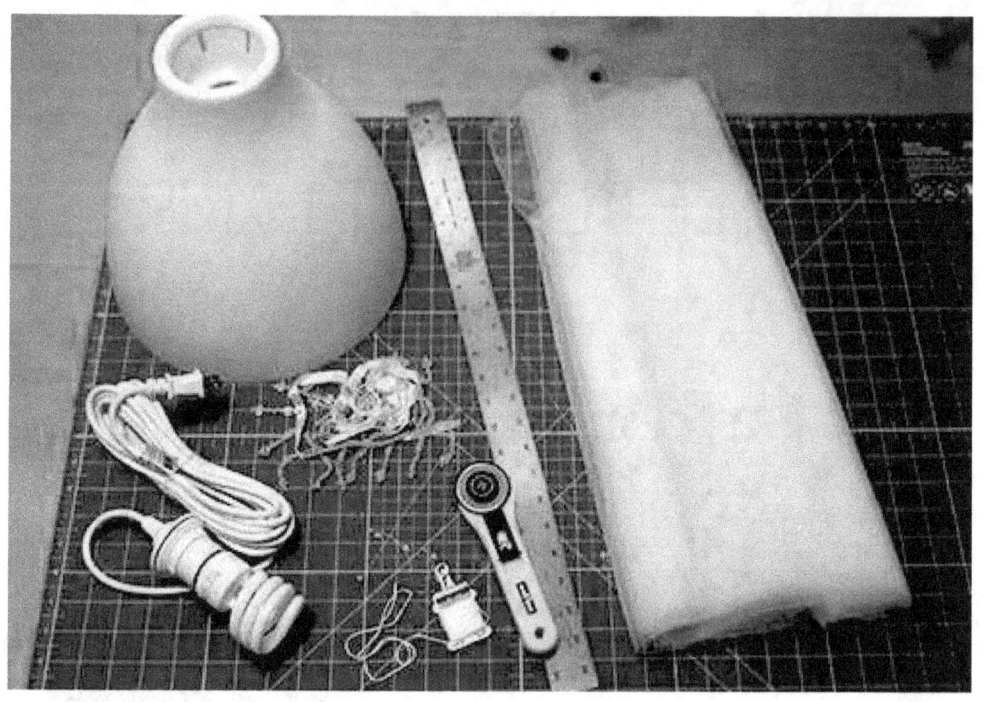

MATERIAL FOR TULLE LAMP

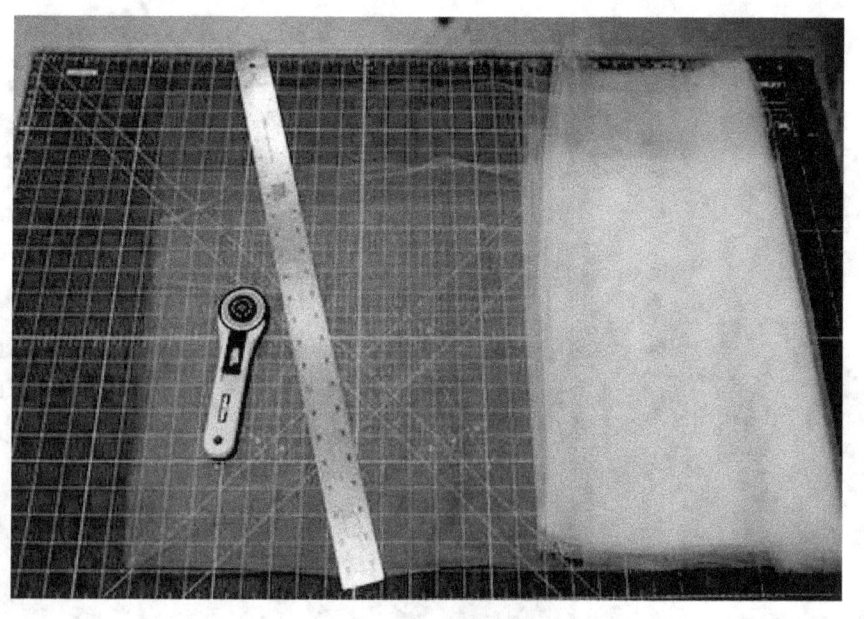

MEASUREMENTS REQUIRED

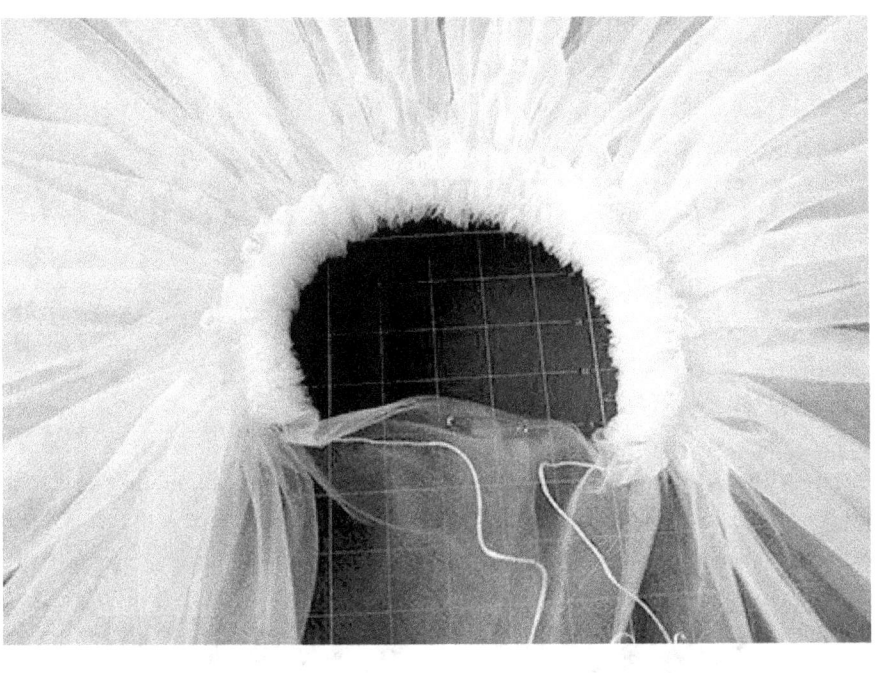

LAMP UPSHADES

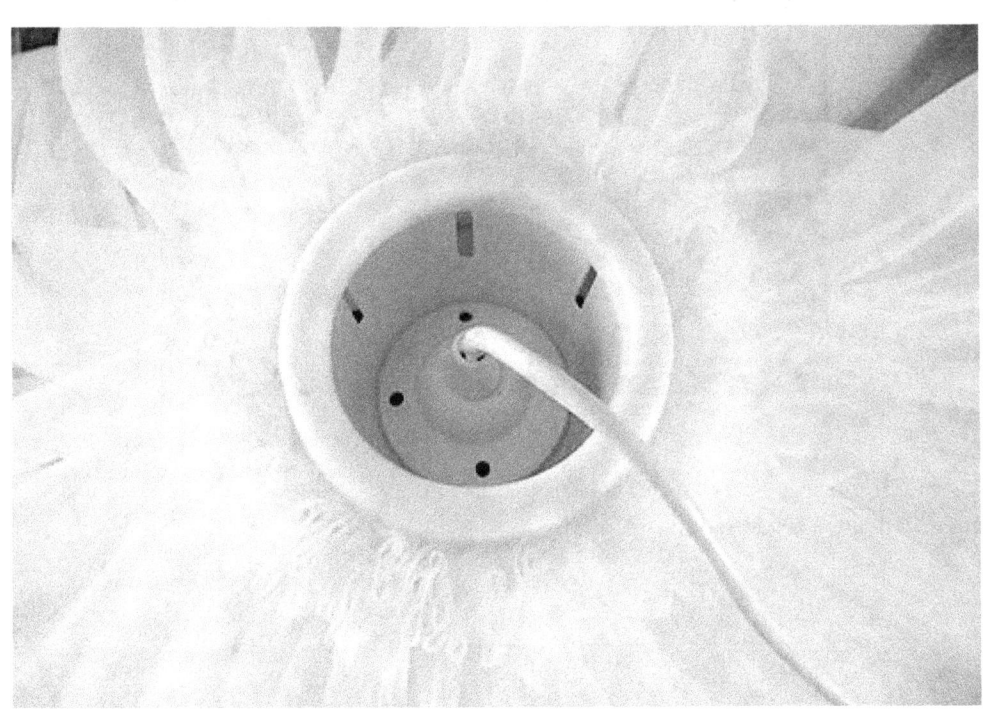

FINAL READY LAMP

BALL THREAD LAMP

BALL THREAD LAMP

Try to make this attractive Thread Lamp shade that gives a perfect look of chandelier to decorate your house, and be ready to see the WOW expression on your guests' face when you will tell them that this Thread Lamp is made by you. This activity is so easy that is perfect to engage kids as young as toddlers.

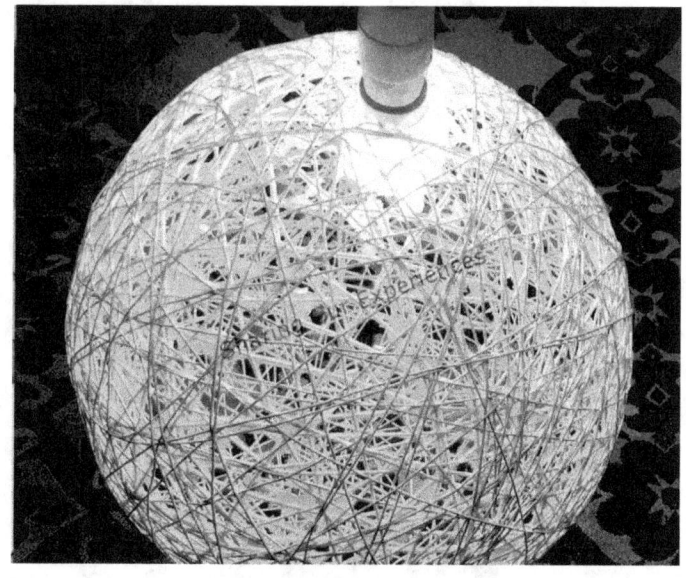

BALL THREAD LAMP

Materials needed to make Thread Lamp
Fevicol
Water
Wool
Air Ball/Balloon
Step 1 – Prepare a mix to soak the wool.

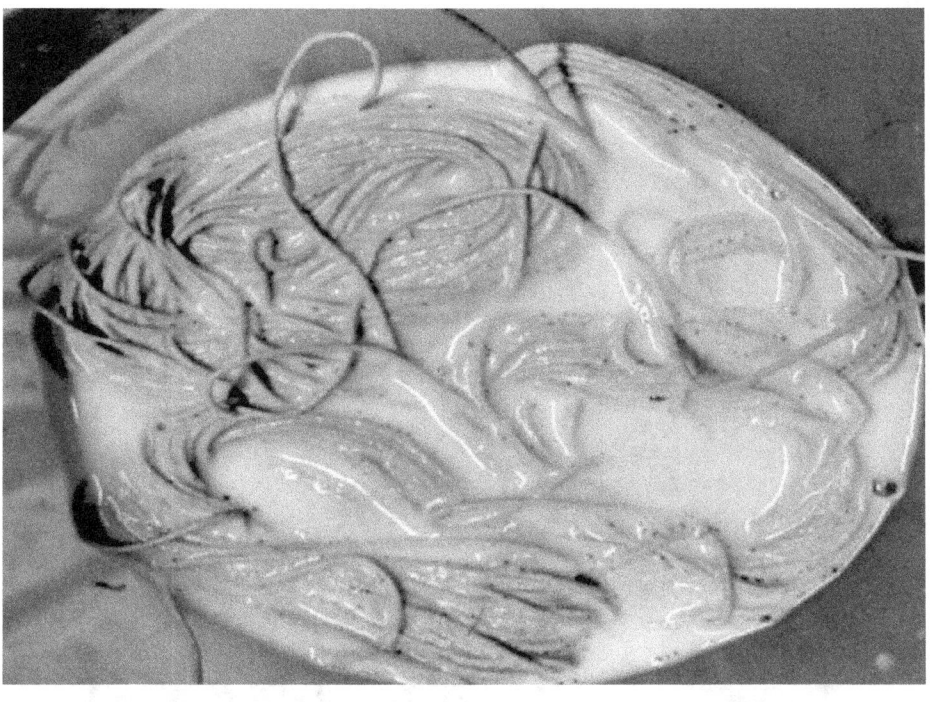

SOAKED WOOL IN FEVICOL

Step 2 – Take a ball or a balloon
Take a ball or balloon, remember to take a ball made of thin material that can be punctured easily at a later point.

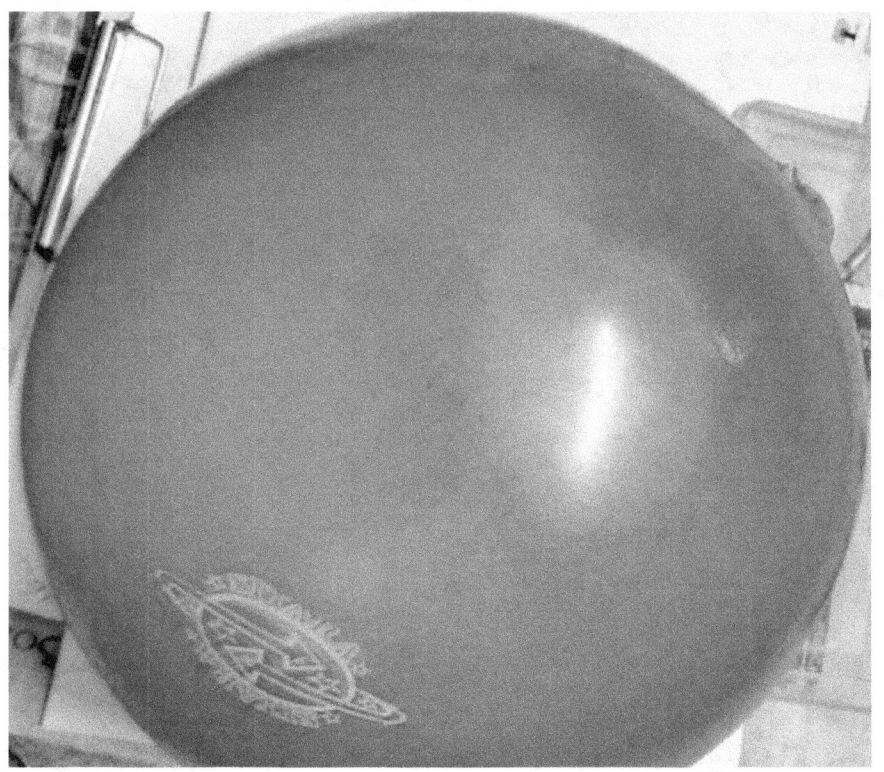

BALL LAMP

Step 3 – Wrap the thread.
Start wrapping the thread (wool) around the ball or balloon to look like a web (shown below)
Note- I have used wool to create the web, you can use rope, string, yarn etc. to weave the web.

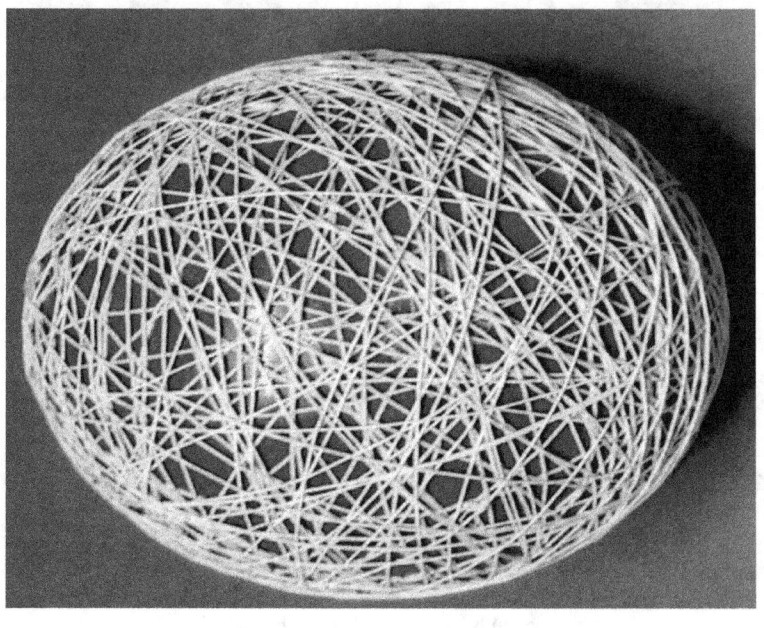

BALL COVERED WITH THREAD

Step 5 – Pinch the ball.
Set it aside for a couple of hours for thread to dry, then pinch the ball or balloon to let the air out of it.

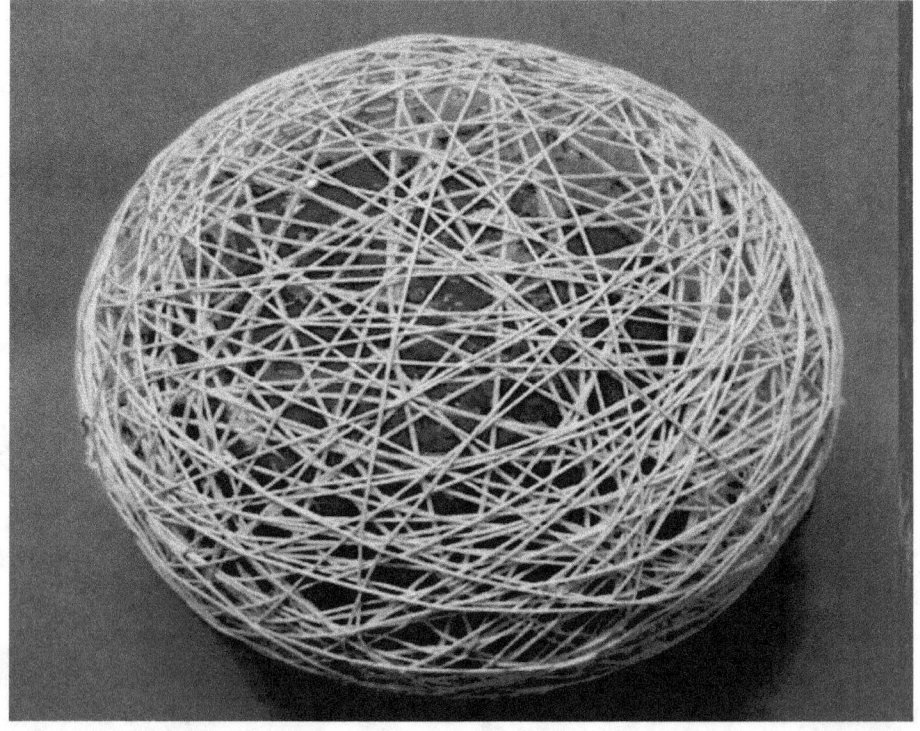

DINFLATE THE BALL

Step 6 – Web is ready.
Take the ball or balloon out from the web.

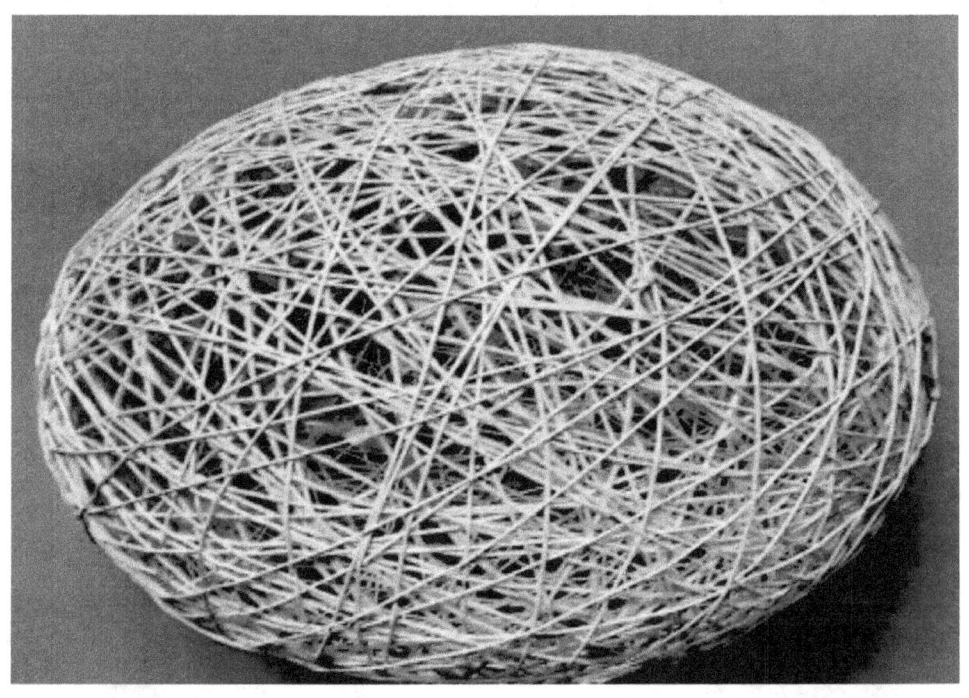

REMOVE THE DEINFLATED BALL

Step 7 – Your woven light shade is ready.

Simply add a light in it and your beautiful chandelier is ready to spread the light. This is a perfect handmade DIY home decoration for festivals like Christmas or Diwali

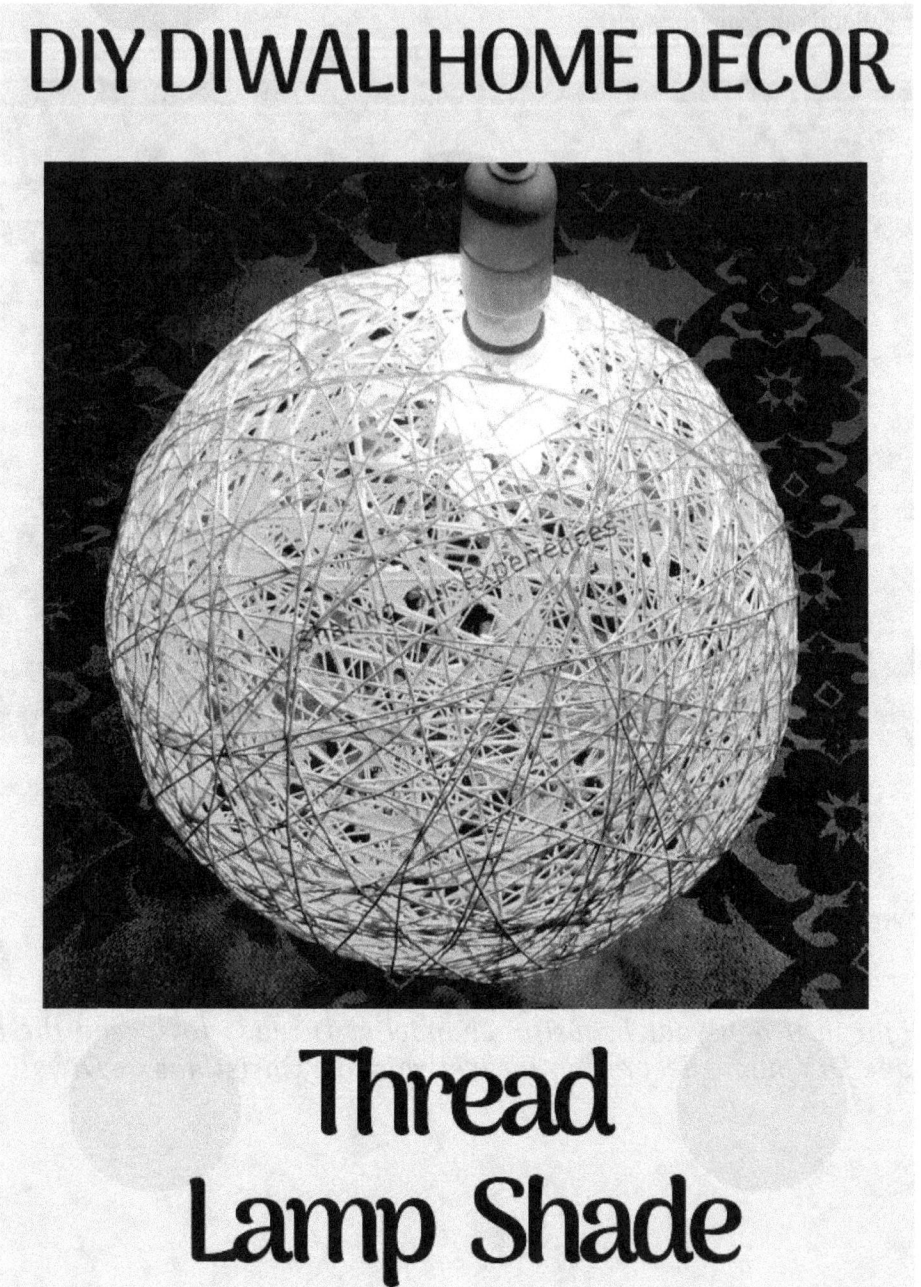

DIY DIWALI HOME DECOR

Thread Lamp Shade

FINAL DECOR LAMP SHADE

Note – You may add different colors in water and fevicol paste to give different color to your lampshade OR simply light bulbs of different colors to make it more beautiful.

CHAPTER SEVEN

PENDANT LIGHT-FISH SCALE

DIY Pendant Light (Fish Scale)

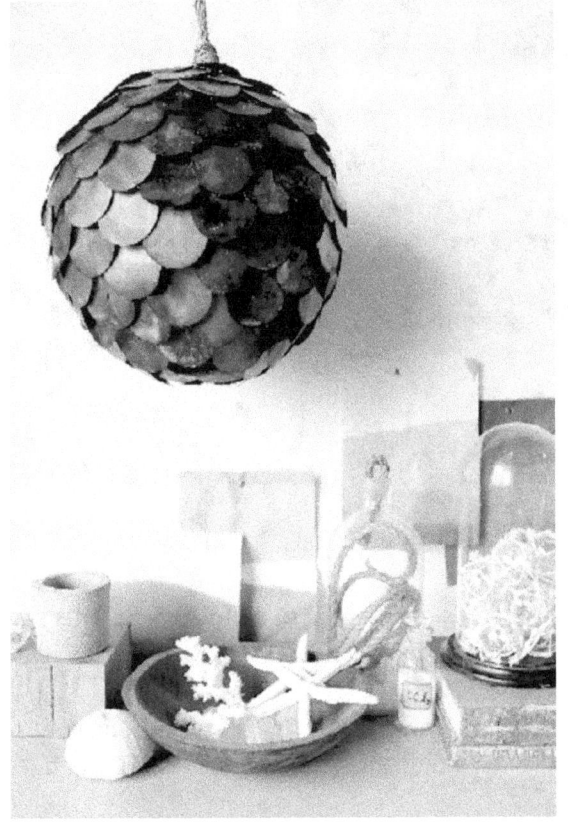

FISH PENDANT LAMP

Here is a fabulous DIY lamp project you can take on with ease! If you like all thing a bit dynamic, this fish scale idea will keep your interest going! Completing this concept will require various elements, such as paper, paraffin wax, mineral oil, crockpot, paper lantern, and a few others. The tutorial itself is simple to follow, while the project will cost you no more than $20. After cutting plenty of circles, you will need to paint them accordingly and let them sit for a while. Then, it is all down to making the pattern work with your plain white lamp! Easy and effective!

CHAPTER EIGHT

RUSTIC LAMP-JUTE LAMP

Rustic Lamp (Jute Wrapped)

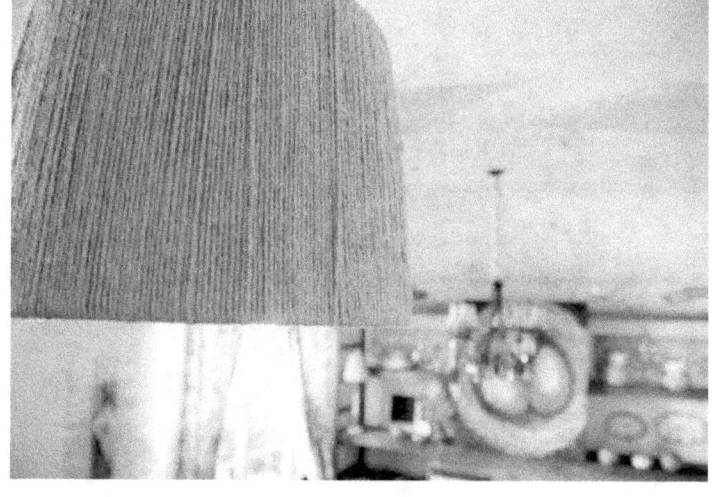

JUTE LAMP

Looking for a change in lighting? Here is a great idea to motivate you. This precious jute-wrapped DIY project is time-friendly, budget-appropriate and cool to have at home! Jute, an old drum light, and some precision are elements needed to carry out the task right.

You will have to keep a stable balance of rope across the lap surface, making sure no cracks or spaces turn up in the end. Although it requires a bit of technique and patience, this DIY lamp doesn't need light to stand out in any room of the house!

CHAPTER NINE

BIRCH TREE HANGING LAMP

Birch Tree Branch Hanging Lamp

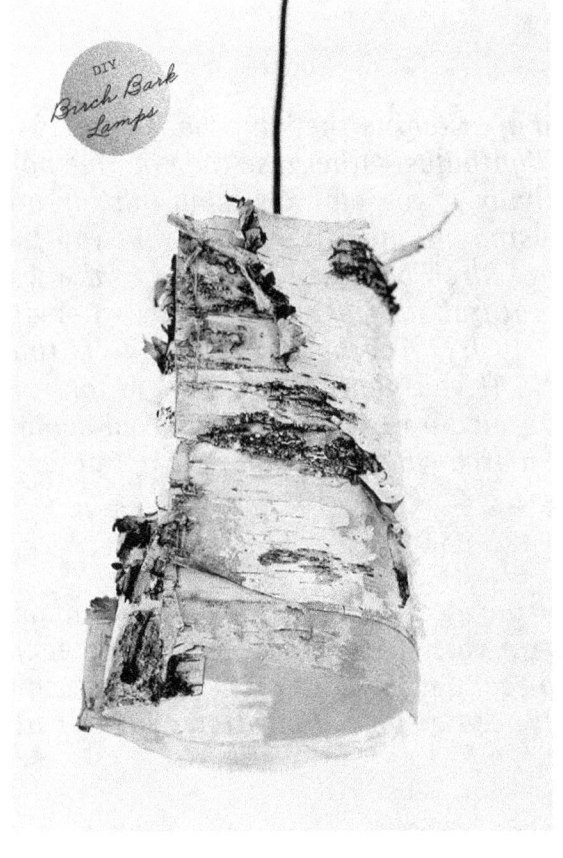

HANGING BIRCH LAMP

READ NEXT
Material Supply list:
.twine or fishing line
.bark
.utility knife
.leather punch
.60 watt lightbulbs
.14 gauge electrical wire and sockets or pendant lamp kits (available at local hardware stores)

One of my brother's neighbors peeled the birch bark off of a dead birch tree he had seen. My friend cut them to the right size i wanted, and using a leather punch cut holes on each end of the "lampshade". He then stitched the ends together with twine.

The lamps were wired together along a really long piece of 14 gauge lamp wire, outfitted with 60 watt incandescent bulbs. The birch bark lampshade was then tied to the pendant wire with the lightbulb suspended in the middle.

A few tips:

You can use hot glue instead of stitching the lampshade ends if you intend to use these them for decoration only without lightbulbs. Otherwise the hot glue bond may eventually loosen up with the heat from the lightbulb. If you plan on using this birch bark lampshade tutorial for your home, we recommend using a lightbulb wattage that you feel makes the most sense for the size shade you'll be using. Birch bark can be found in the woods, and it's free! If you're getting birch bark from its natural source, rinse it with water and a splash of bleach before you bring it indoors, and let it dry. Another thing to note is that over time, birch bark will eventually dry out and crack. If you plan on using them for your house, consider applying a coat of acrylic clear matte medium. It's a water based sealant, and it won't yellow like polyurethane. If you live in an area where birch bark is not accessible, you can purchase birch veneer sheets anywhere online.

If you're not familiar with wiring electrical cords, I recommend using pendant lamp kits. Each lamp will be lit independently, which means you could hang each lamp above a table! If you like these lamps but prefer a seamless look to them, you can use nylon fishing line instead of twine. Table lampshades will need a spider top fitter, available at lamp shade part stores like this one.

Using the same instructions + tips, you can use birch bark to wrap containers to use as centerpieces, make napkin rings, and votive holders! We'd love to see what you come up with!

CHAPTER TEN

Birch Bark Lamp For A Chic Rustic Touch

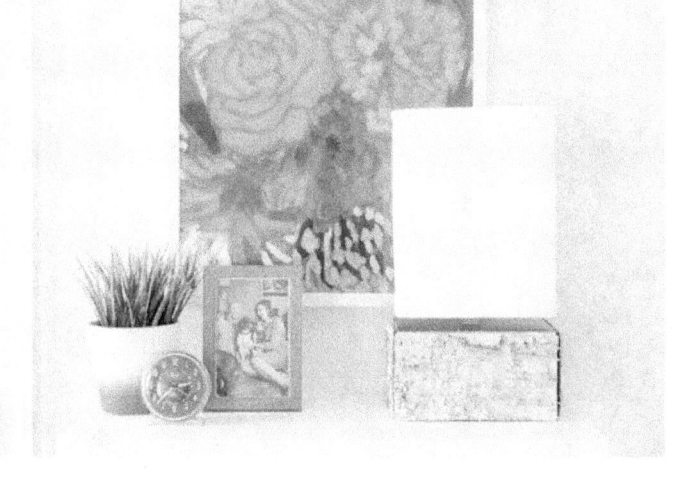

RUSTIC BIRCH LAMP

It's easy to give a modern, rectangular table lamp a rustic makeover using sheets of pliable birch bark to get a bit of cabin chic. The supplies are a table lamp, sheets of bendable birch bark, a ruler, a marker or pen, heavy duty sheers, removable, double-sided adhesive strips, twine and scissors. Use a ruler to measure the height and width of the sides of your table lamp. Measure and make marks with a marker or pen on the birch bark sheets to correspond with the measurements of the table lamp base. Use heavy duty sheers to slowly cut through the birch bark sheets. Make sure to carefully follow the measured pen marks made in the previous step.

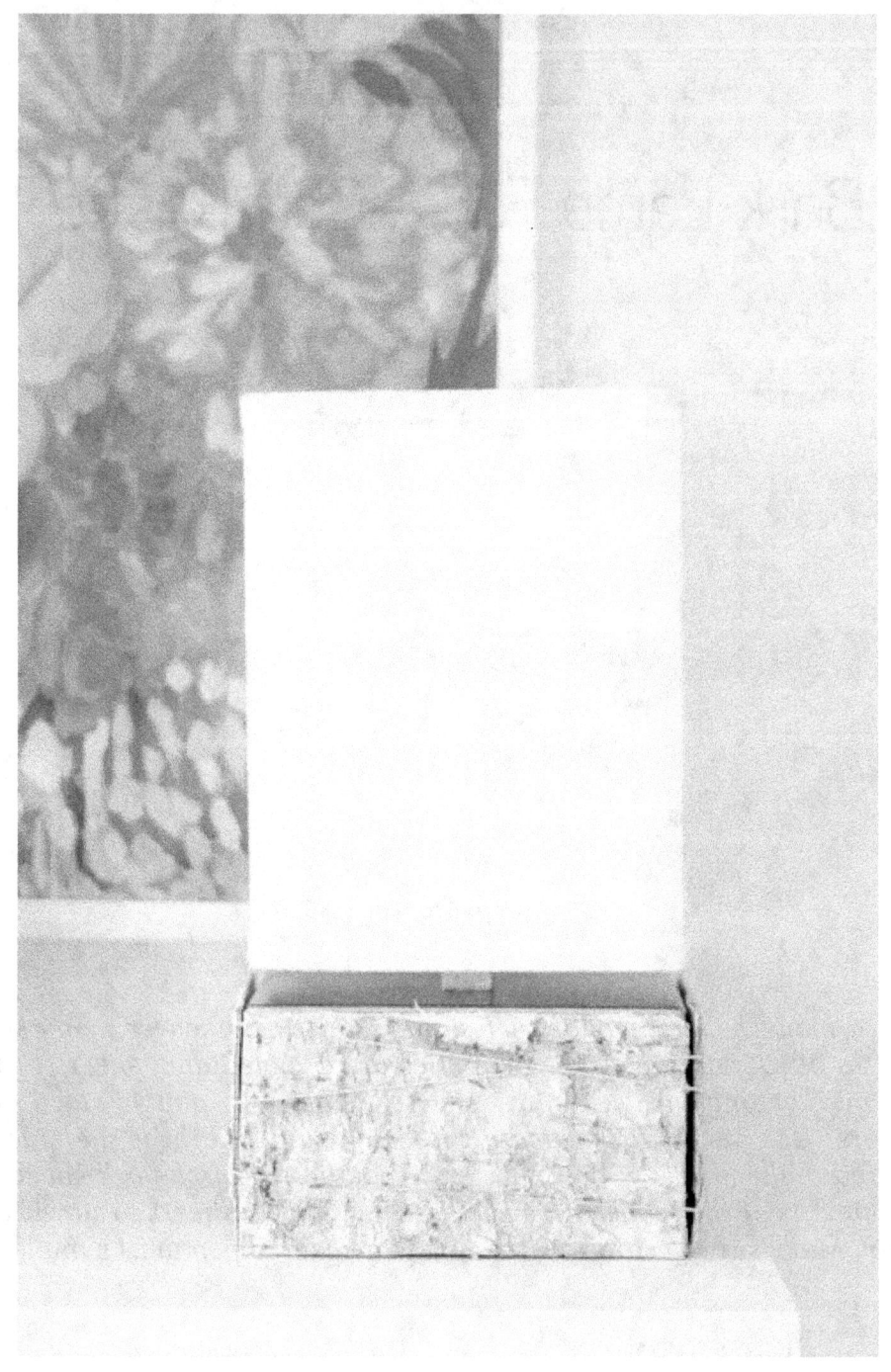

ATTRACTIVE SIMPLE,EASY TO MAKE

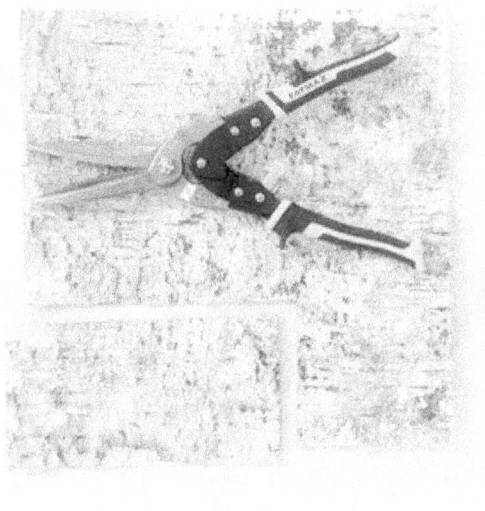

CUT WODDEN BIRCH IN A RECTANGULAR FORM WITH A PLIER

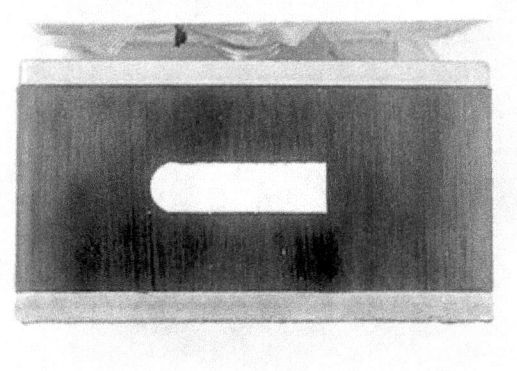

COVER WOODEM RECTANGULAR CUBOID WITH THE WOODEN PLANKS

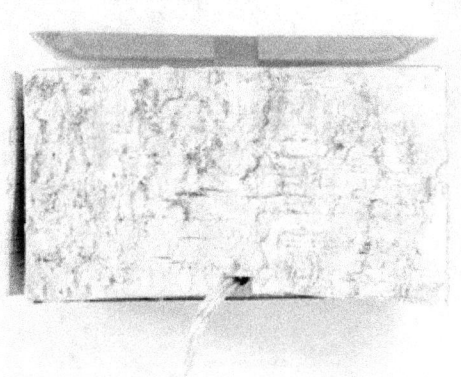

COVER ALL SIDES OF CUBOID WITH WOODEN PLANKS

HOLD TIGHTLY ,TIE THE PLANKS WITH STRONG THREAD

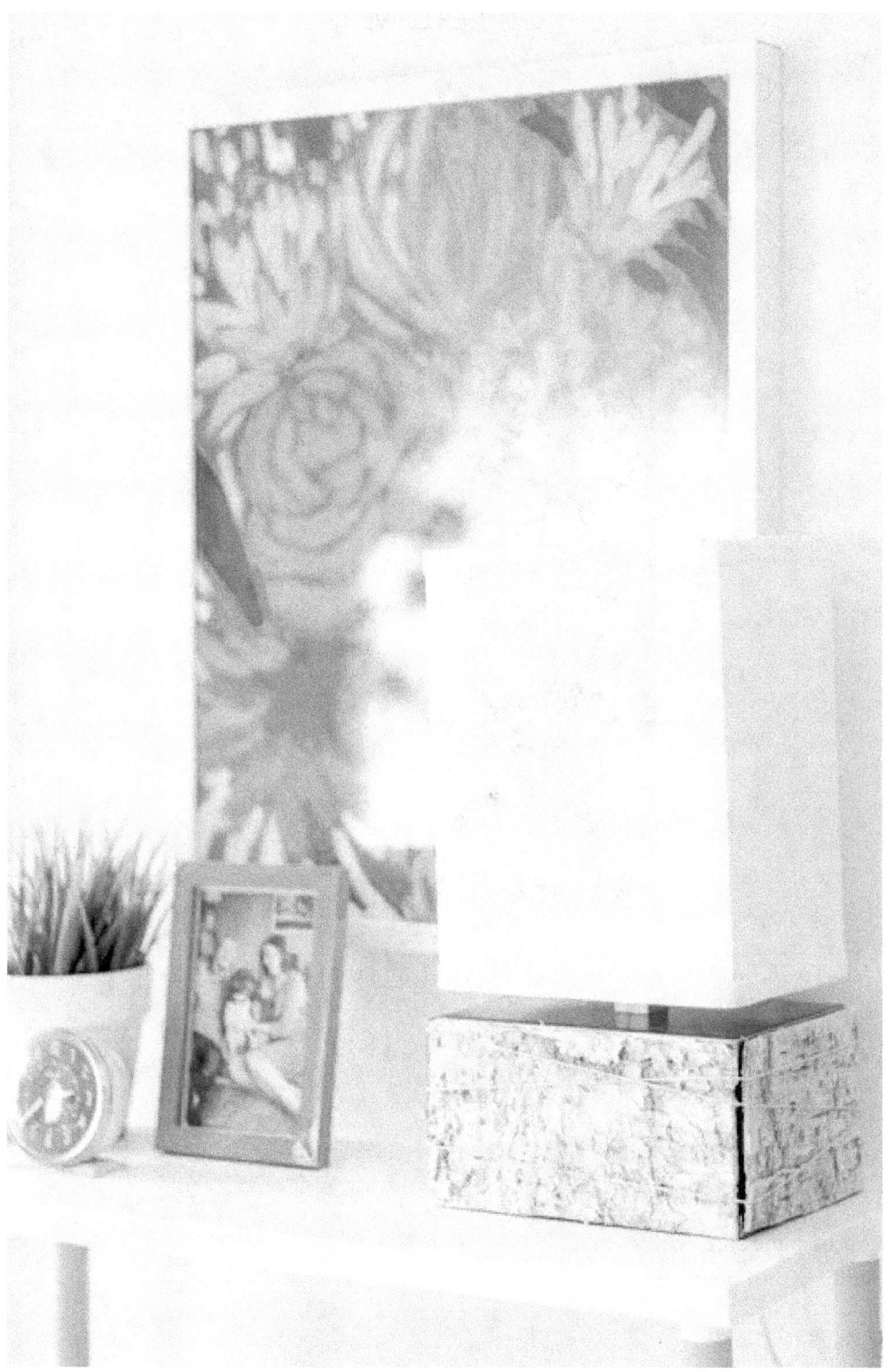

NOW MAKE FINAL ARRANGEMENT WITH A TOP LAMP SHADE ADDED WITH THE SOCKET & BULB ARRANGEMENT

CHAPTER ELEVEN

VINTAGE FANS

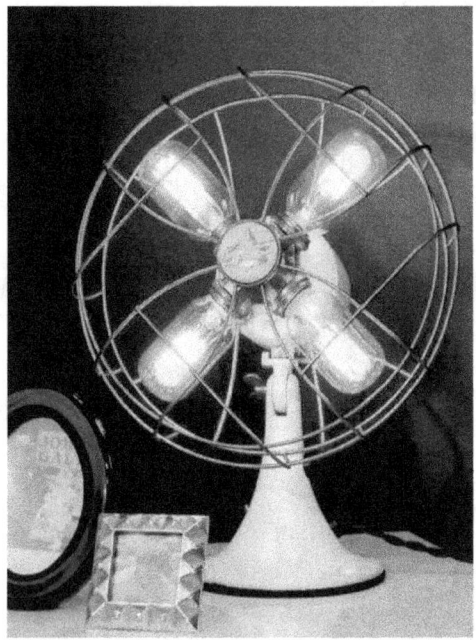

FAN VINTAGE LAMPFlea Market Lighting Fan Lamp with Edison Light Bulbs by Do it yourself:

Materials

.Fan
  .3 way light socket
  .Eidson bulbs
  .Lamp wiring kit of some sort, with switch.
  .Brass spray paint

Directions

1) Take apart the fan. Remove wiring and separate the cage spray paint all hardware
   2) Insert lamp kit into fan
   3) Spray paint inside parts, brass or copper
   4) Wire the lighting into the fan so the plug comes out the bottom
   5) Put the cage back on.
   6) Put bulbs into the light socket and screw in the 3-socket splitter

CHAPTER TWELVE

Old Kettle Pendant Lamp

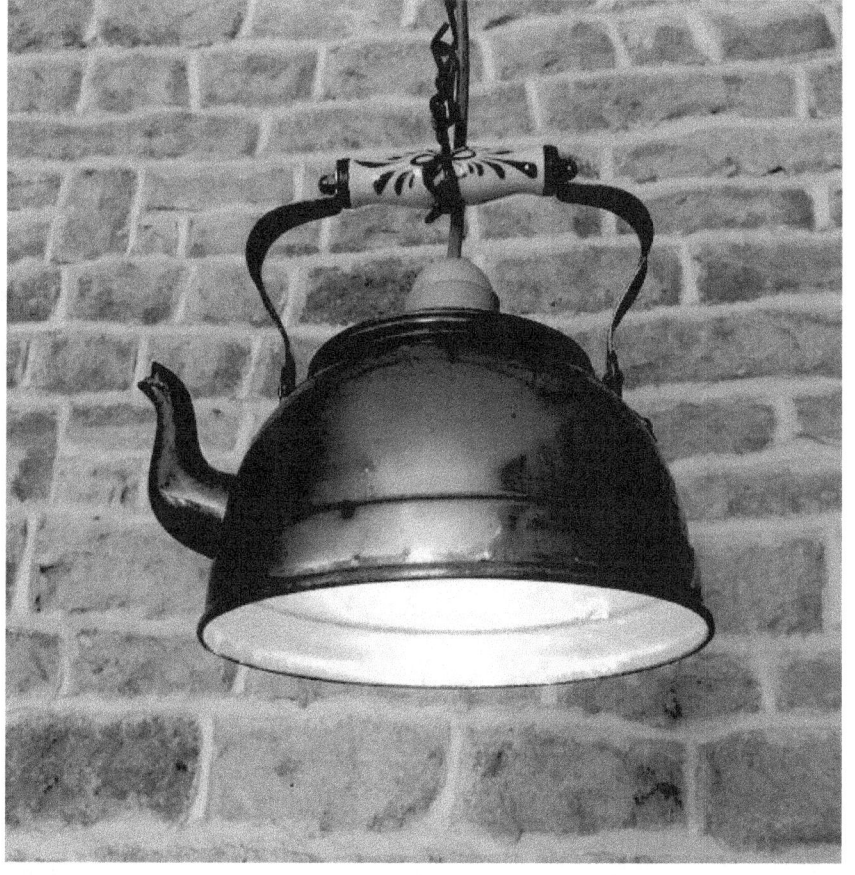

TEA KETTLE LAMP

Love this old copper kettle lamp made by removing the base & adding the bulb & socket fitting in side it.

Amazing replacement ,Just add the fittings with electric illumination system,Hang it ovearhead on the ceiling.For amazing results use Edision Bulbs.......

CHAPTER THIRTEEN

Living Lamp Terrarium

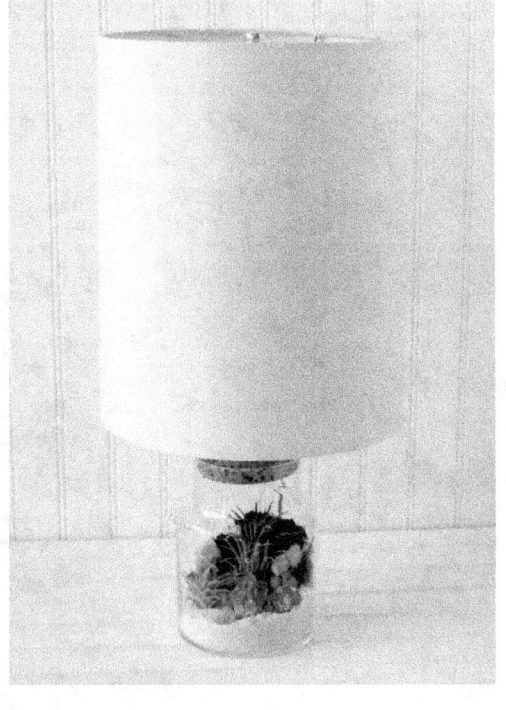

TERRARIUM LAMP

This DIY Terrarium Lamp is a great project for small spaces. Adding a little light, and a little green and an easy way to brighten up your home. You will find that adding air plants and moss to your terrarium is the most minimalist of ways to care for plants. All you need to do is find a glass jug or clear container with a lid and glue the lamp stem to the top. This way, you can still remove the lid to have access to your plants.

What you need

Lamp kit (purchase at any hardware store)

Lamp shade

Light bulb

Clear glass container with removable lid

glue gun, or stronger glue such as E6000

Air plants

Moss

Sand

Small rocks

Small gems or minerals

Instructions
Gather supplies:

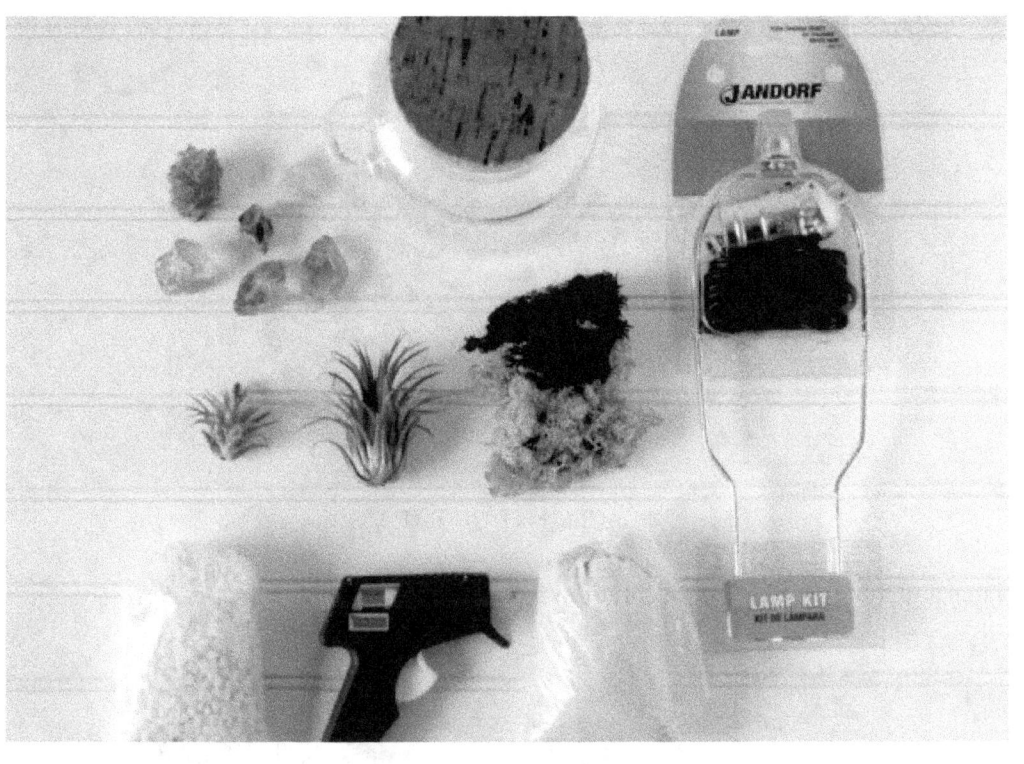

KIT TO MAKE LAMP

1. Add sand and rocks

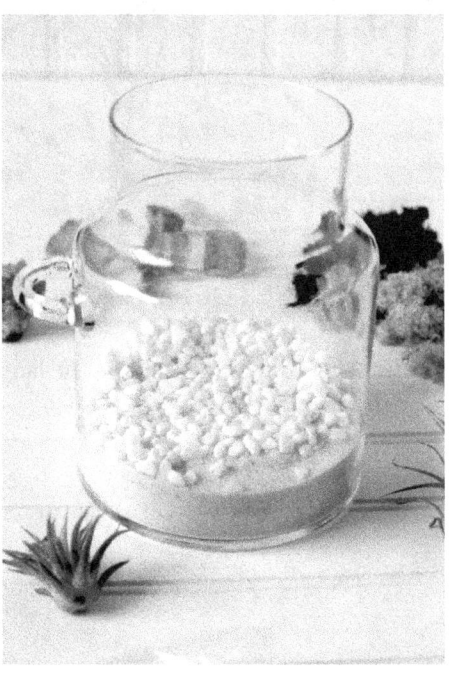

PLACEMENT OF THE BASE

2) Add colorful moss to the background.

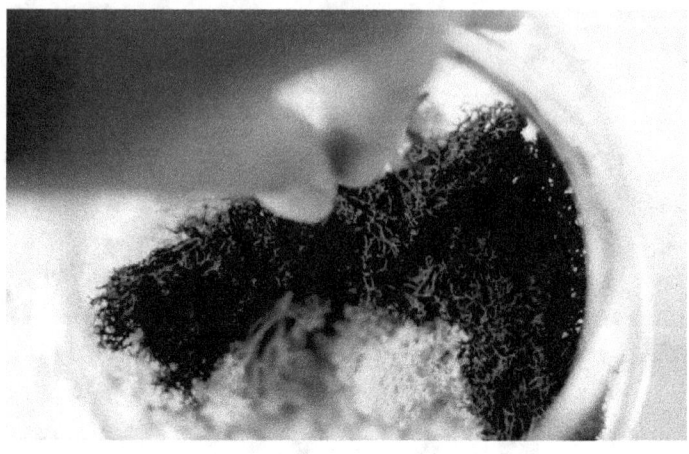

PLACEMENT OF THE MOSS

3. Add air plants and minerals or other decorations to the foreground of the landscape

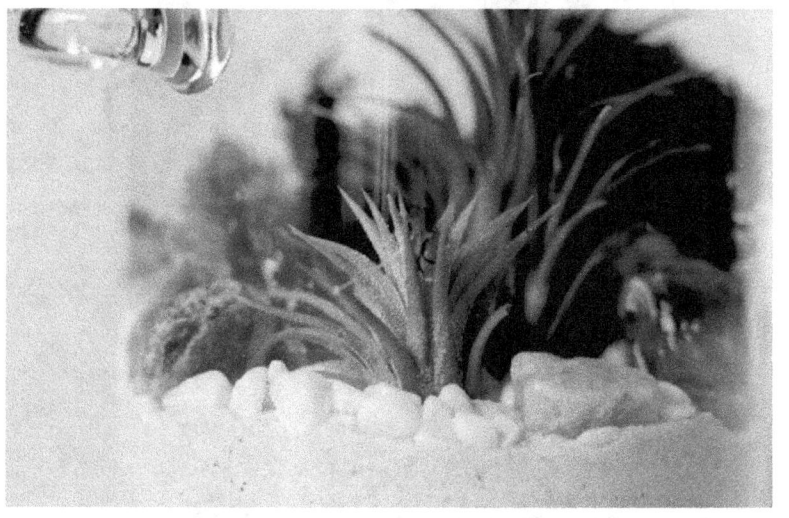

SETTLEMENT OF LANDSCAPING

4. Follow the instructions that accompany your lamp kit, assemble the lamp, and add the light bulb

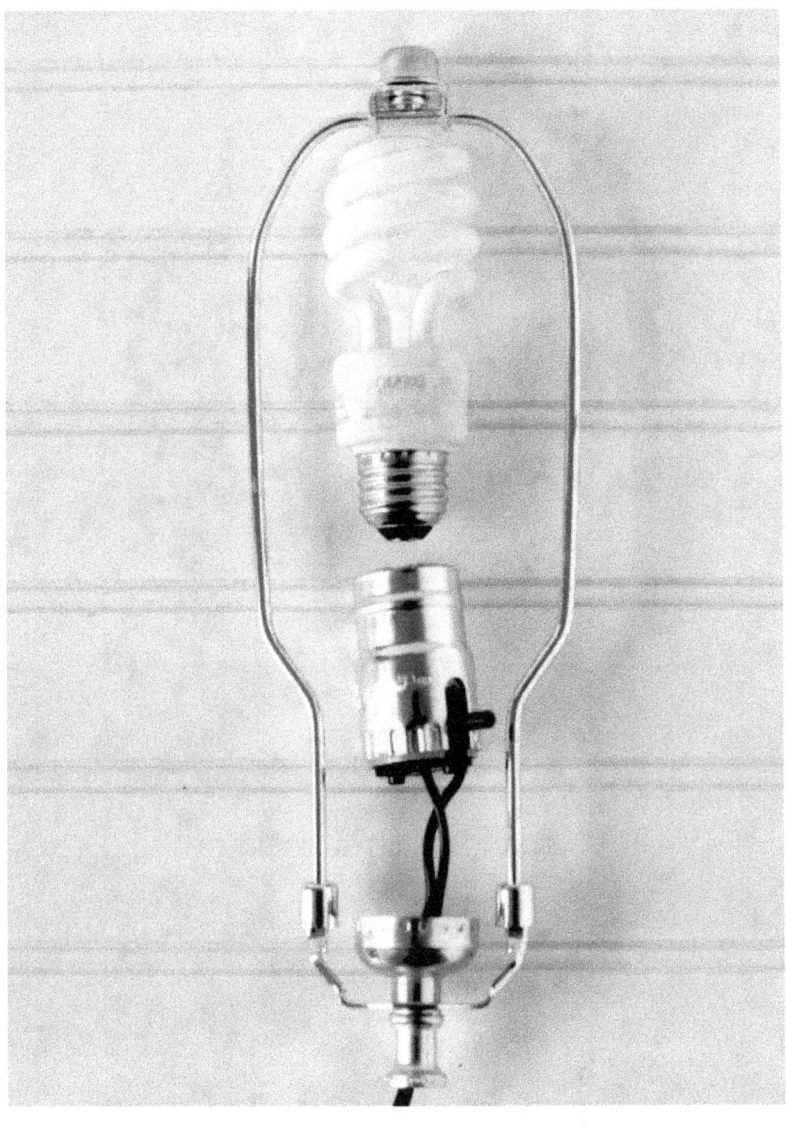

ATTACHEMENT OF SOCKET JUNCTION

5. Glue the base of the lamp to the top lid of your container. I used a hot glue gun, but you may want to use stronger bonding glue depending on your lid. I found the hot glue to be a little flimsy so I reinforced it using stronger craft glue (E6000 glue).

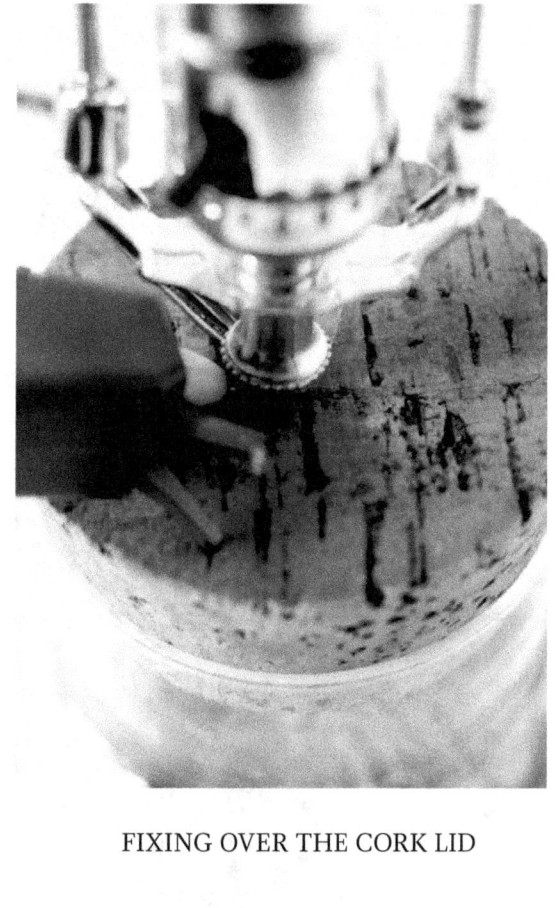

FIXING OVER THE CORK LID

6. Add your lamp shade

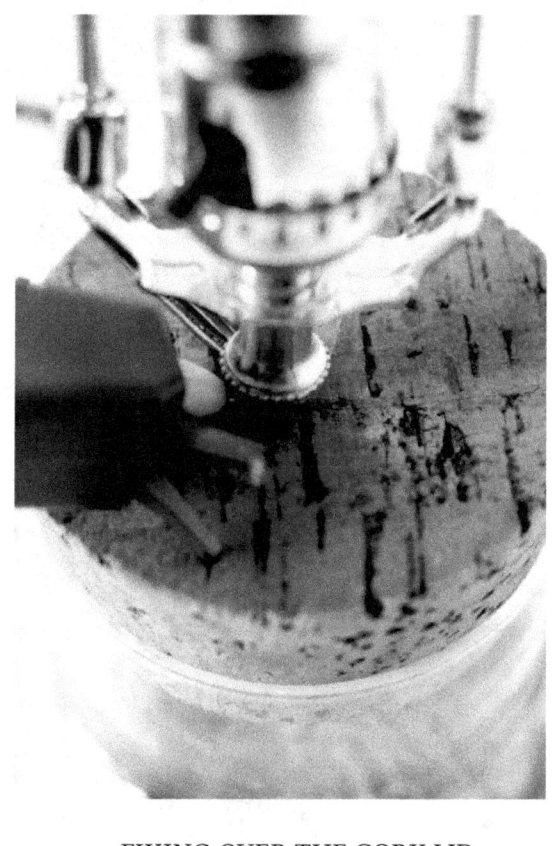

FIXING THE LAMPSHADE

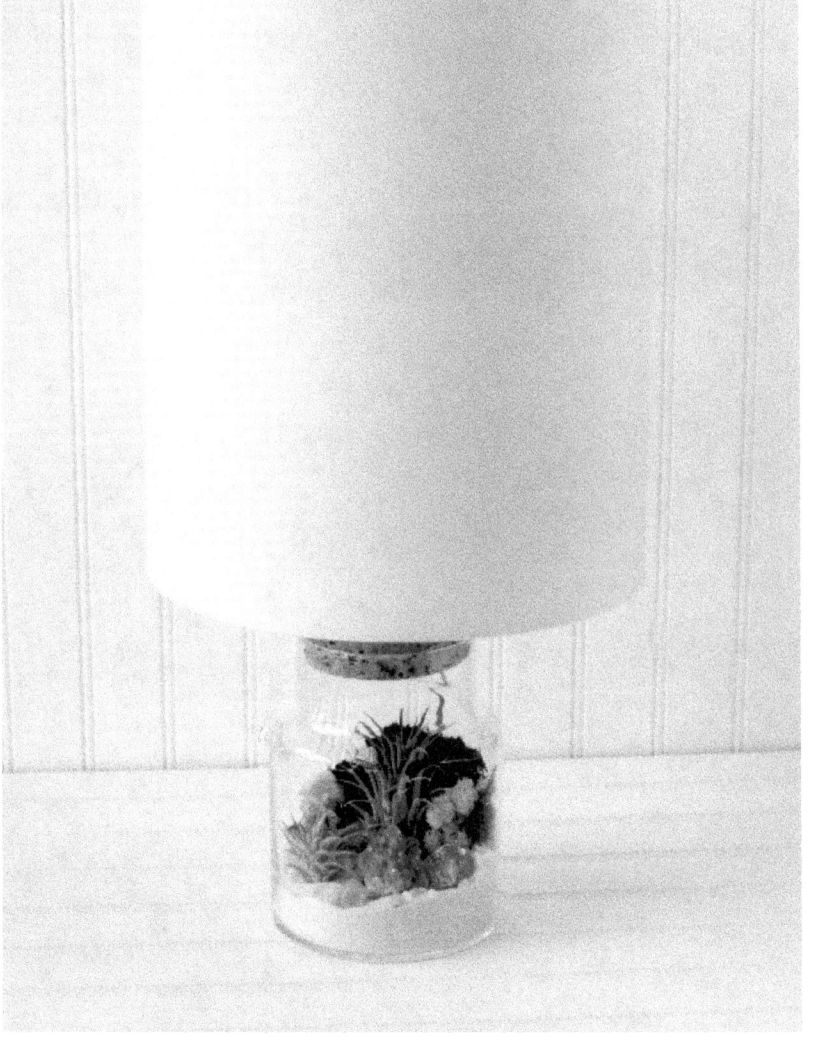

HANDMADE TERRARIUM LAMP FINALLY